Where Were the Seven Wonders of the Ancient World?

by Yona Zeldis McDonough

illustrated by Dede Putra

Penguin Workshop

For Jane O'Connor—
great editor, great lady!
—YZM

PENGUIN WORKSHOP
An Imprint of Penguin Random House LLC, New York

Visit us online at www.penguinrandomhouse.com.

Library of Congress Control Number: 2019038773

ISBN 9780593093306 (paperback)   10 9 8 7 6 5 4 3 2
ISBN 9780593093313 (library binding)   10 9 8 7 6 5 4 3 2 1

Contents

ROME

TEMPLE OF
ARTEMIS

GREECE

EPHESUS

OLYMPIA

MAUSOLEUM AT
HALICARNASSUS

STATUE
OF ZEUS

RHODES

COLOSSUS
OF RHODES

MEDITERRANEAN SEA

LIGHTHOUSE
OF ALEXANDRIA

ALEXANDRIA

GIZA

GREAT PYRAMID
AT GIZA

NILE RIVER

EGYPT

Where Were the Seven Wonders of the Ancient World?

Imagine you live thousands of years ago, somewhere in the area you see on the map. Even back then, people wanted to travel and see the world's most famous landmarks. Several writers from ancient times did just that.

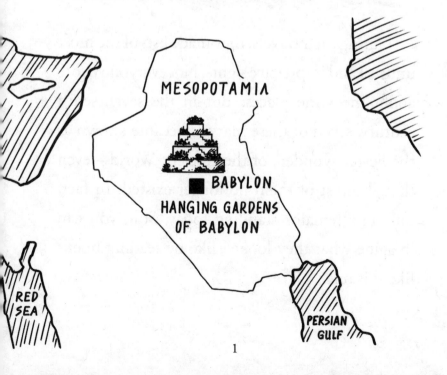

MESOPOTAMIA

BABYLON
HANGING GARDENS
OF BABYLON

RED
SEA

PERSIAN
GULF

During their travels, they made lists of the most unusual and impressive sights. Not everyone wrote about the same places. But in the seventeenth century, seven of these marvels became known as the Seven Wonders of the Ancient World—even though most of them no longer existed. In fact, only one remains standing today. Still, you can imagine what they looked like by reading books like this one.

CHAPTER 1
The Great Pyramid at Giza

Perhaps the most famous monument in the world is the Great Pyramid at Giza in northern Egypt. (A pyramid is a three-dimensional object with triangular sides that meet in a point at the top.) That's because it's so huge and old, and the story of why and how it was built is so interesting.

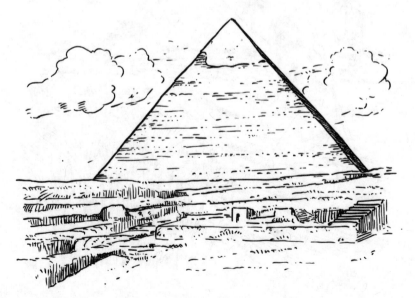

The pyramid at Giza was built by the Egyptians during the years 2550–2530 BC. Egypt was a great civilization even more than 4,500 years ago. The Egyptians were able to build a pyramid as tall as a fifty-story skyscraper. At its base, each side is about 756 feet long. That's more than twice the length of a football field.

For longer than 3,880 years, the Great Pyramid remained the tallest structure made by human hands in the entire world—that's quite a record!

Unlike all the other ancient wonders in this book, the Great Pyramid is still standing. It is located outside the city of Cairo, on the Nile River.

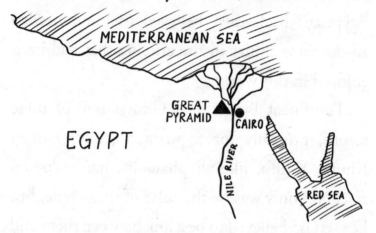

It's made of over two million blocks of limestone and granite. Some of the blocks are so big and heavy that even today, no one knows exactly how builders in ancient times were able to put them in place. They are not held together with mortar (mortar is like concrete). Instead, the blocks fit next to one another so perfectly that the pyramid has stood for 4,500 years.

We know a lot about life in ancient Egypt because good records were kept and because so many objects—both practical things and works of art—were put in the tombs for the dead. Egyptians back then believed the soul needed all the same things in the afterlife that had been enjoyed in this world.

The Great Pyramid at Giza is one of these tombs, probably for a pharaoh (ruler) named Khufu. Khufu, like all pharaohs, had a special role. Not only was he the ruler of the people, but he was also believed to be a link between them and the gods. By performing certain ceremonies, the pharaoh made sure that the sun would rise and set, the Nile River would flow, and the crops would grow. And when the king died, he became a god. For this reason, everything about his death and burial was considered extremely important.

Khufu

Khufu (say: COO-foo) was about twenty years old when he became pharaoh in 2589 BC. He ruled for a long time—more than twenty years. His full name, Khnum-khufu,

means "Khnum protects me." Khnum was one of many gods the Egyptians worshipped. Khnum was the ram-headed god of the earth, creation, and growth. Khufu had several wives, which was common in ancient times. He had nine sons and fifteen daughters, and gave them all high positions in the royal court. Khufu was known as an evil leader who was feared and hated by his people.

After Khufu's death, his body was made into a mummy and put inside a highly decorated, body-shaped coffin. That coffin was then put into a sarcophagus (a stone coffin). Deep within Khufu's pyramid, secret tunnels

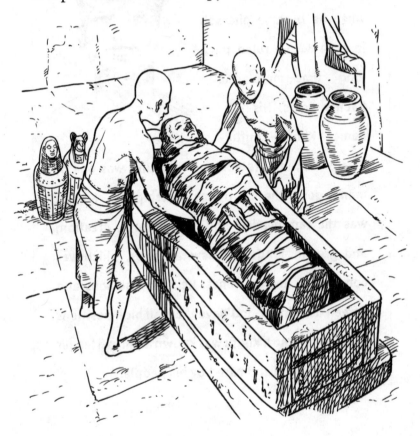

led to a room where his sarcophagus would have been surrounded by food, beautiful furniture, board games, precious jewelry, and so on. It was believed that his soul would rest in the chamber for eternity and, because of this, Egypt would thrive. Today, nothing remains inside the Great Pyramid. Why? Most likely robbers in ancient times broke in and looted all the treasure.

So we know what the Great Pyramid was for. We also know who built it. For many years, it was believed that slave labor was used to construct the pyramid. But that's not true. Although there were enslaved people in ancient Egypt, the pyramid at Giza was built by paid workers, hired by the pharaoh.

During the time when the land and fields were flooded by the Nile, farming was impossible. So a lot of men were available to work. It's believed that twenty to thirty thousand men were employed in the pyramid's construction.

Egyptian Gods and Goddesses

Ancient Egyptians worshipped a huge number of gods and goddesses.

Some of them looked human. Others were part human and part animal. Still others looked entirely like animals—crocodiles, jackals, cats, rams, and falcons. Here are some of the more famous ones:

- Osiris—Ruler of the underworld and the judge of the dead
- Set, or Seth—God of darkness, destruction, and chaos
- Isis—Wife of Osiris and goddess of healing, motherhood, and the protection of children
- Thoth—God of science, logic, intelligence, knowledge, writing, and reason. He had the head of an ibis, a bird with a curved beak.

- **Anubis**—Jackal-headed god of the dead, tombs, and embalming
- **Sobek**—Crocodile god of strength, medicine, and power
- **Bastet**—Warrior goddess in the form of a cat
- **Horus**—God of the sky
- **Ra**—Sun god
- **Hathor**—Goddess of love, beauty, music, laughter, and fun

Ra, sun god

The question of *how* the pyramid was built is much harder to answer. The huge stones were probably cut from quarries close to the Nile. Then big boats might have transported each block of stone to the site of the pyramid. One theory says wooden ramps ran around the outside of the structure, going higher and higher.

Perhaps the blocks were dragged up the ramps by gangs of men and put into place. It's possible, but we can't be sure.

According to an ancient historian, building the pyramid took thirty years. Ten of those years were just to get ready—preparing the site, building roads and homes for the workers, removing the stone from quarries.

The workers used copper and bronze metal tools, sleds (carts on runners pulled by animals) ropes, rollers, and levers. They didn't have iron or steel tools, steam shovels, dump trucks, or cranes—none of the things that are used in the modern construction of tall buildings. That alone makes building the Great Pyramid remarkable.

Once the Great Pyramid was completed, the facade (the outer surface) was covered in white limestone, which would have shone brilliantly and been visible from every direction for miles around. A capstone, probably covered in a layer of gold, was placed at the top. A capstone is a small pyramid at the point at which the triangular sides meet. What an astonishing sight it must have been!

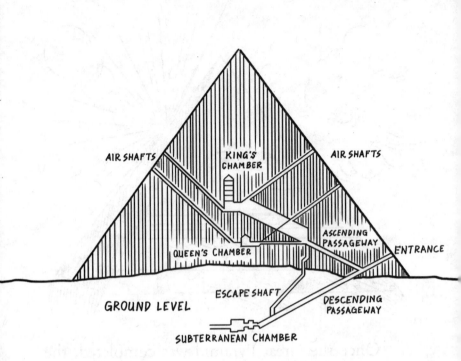

Cross section of the interior of the Great Pyramid of Khufu

Inside the Great Pyramid there are three known chambers. The lowest chamber was never finished. The so-called Queen's Chamber and King's Chamber are higher up within the pyramid structure. The inner rooms and walls are made of polished granite, one of the hardest stones known in Khufu's time.

Alongside the pyramid at Giza are two temples, and a raised causeway, or road, to connect them. There are also places to leave food and other offerings for the dead pharaoh. One was close to the pyramid and the other was near the Nile River.

The area includes other smaller pyramids, known as the Queens' Pyramids. Three remain standing at almost full height. They were built for other wives and sisters of the pharaoh.

The Queens' Pyramids

Another was almost entirely buried in the sand and discovered by accident. It was built for Khufu's mother.

In addition, the complex has mastabas (say: MAS-tuh-buhz), which are much smaller flat-topped tombs built for Egyptian nobles.

Following Khufu's death, his son became king and began building his own pyramid next to his father's. Khufu's grandson also built his eternal home at Giza. Both these pharaohs added their own temples and other monuments, such as the Great Sphinx of Giza. Still, neither of their tombs ever rose to the height of the Great Pyramid. Most likely, that would have pleased Khufu!

The pyramid of Khufu's grandson

The Sphinx

The Great Sphinx is a colossal statue carved from limestone. It has the head of a man and the body of a lion. It's believed to be a guardian figure, meant to protect the tomb and keep evil away.

For thousands of years, money was set aside for Giza's upkeep. But after Alexander the Great conquered Egypt in 332 BC and founded a new city called Alexandria, the pyramids at Giza began to fall into ruin.

The Great Pyramid was first fully excavated by a professional archaeologist between 1880 and 1882. (To excavate means to dig out a hole, sometimes in order to expose something that's buried.) Sir William Matthew Flinders Petrie

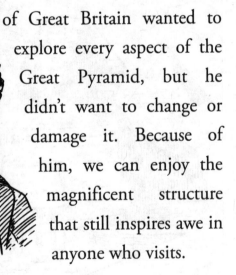

of Great Britain wanted to explore every aspect of the Great Pyramid, but he didn't want to change or damage it. Because of him, we can enjoy the magnificent structure that still inspires awe in anyone who visits.

Sir William Matthew Flinders Petrie

CHAPTER 2
The Hanging Gardens of Babylon

Two thousand five hundred years ago, Egypt was no longer the power it once had been. At this time, the largest and most magnificent city in the world was Babylon in a country known as Babylonia. (That's in present-day Iraq.)

Babylon was famous for three things. One was a temple to the god Marduk. For the Babylonians, Marduk was the chief god.

Marduk

Temple to Marduk

The city walls of Babylon were another marvel. More than ten miles of wall enclosed the city. They were so wide that two chariots, each pulled by four horses, could pass each other on top of them.

The third famous landmark in Babylon was the fabled Hanging Gardens. They were built by King Nebuchadnezzar II (say: neh-byuh-kuhd-NEHZ-er). He ruled from 605 BC to 561 BC.

The name of the gardens is confusing. They

didn't actually hang in midair. They were built high above the ground on multilevel stone terraces within the palace walls. But from a distance, the gardens must have looked like they were floating, green and beautiful, above the dry, dusty city below.

According to legend, the king had them built to cheer up his wife, Queen Amytis (say: AH-mee-tiss). She had come from another land and was the daughter of a king. She married Nebuchadnezzar to create a strong bond between their two nations.

King Nebuchadnezzar II and Queen Amytis

But Amytis didn't like her new country. Not at all. It was flat, dry, and hot. She missed the green valleys and hills where she'd grown up. Nebuchadnezzar hoped that the gardens would remind her of home.

The hanging gardens were laid out in a giant square—400 feet wide by 400 feet long. That's even bigger than a city block. They rose more than 80 feet high—that's taller than a six-story building. The base of the garden was made of huge slabs of stone, tiles, asphalt (which is used in streets today), and reeds. It was deep enough that roots of big trees would have room to grow. Besides trees, there were shrubs, flowers, and vines planted in the gardens. There were also man-made streams, fountains, and waterfalls. Wild animals roamed freely. Greek and Roman travelers described it as a magical and enchanting place . . . even though none of them had actually seen it themselves.

One of many mysteries about the gardens is understanding how they were watered. Water would have to have been carried all the way to the topmost garden. And the gardens are estimated to have needed 8,200 gallons of water every day. To accomplish that would have been an amazing engineering feat, especially in ancient times.

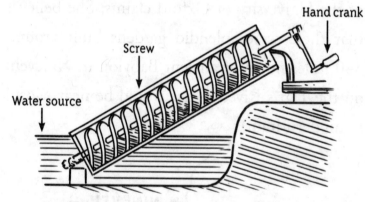

Possible technique for watering the Hanging Gardens

King Nebuchadnezzar didn't leave any records about how this was done. And although there are hundreds of documents describing many of his other building projects, there isn't a single one about any gardens.

In fact, it's entirely possible that the Hanging Gardens of Babylon may not have existed at all. Clay tablets from the time don't mention them. Nor have any archaeological digs in the area turned up evidence of them.

But maybe the gardens *did* exist—only not in the city of Babylon. That's what Stephanie Dalley of the University of Oxford claims. She believes that there were splendid gardens built around 340 miles north of ancient Babylon in Nineveh, on the Tigris River. (That would be near Mosul in modern Iraq.)

If that is true, the gardens would have been created by a different king who ruled one hundred years before Nebuchadnezzar. His name was Sennacherib (say: sen-NAH-keh-rib). He turned Nineveh into a magnificent city.

Sennacherib

A system of eighteen canals, roughly fifty miles long, brought water from the hills to Nineveh. Given the scale of Sennacherib's many grand projects, it's possible that he could have designed and built the Hanging Gardens.

And we have Sennacherib's own words: *I planted a great park beside the palace . . . with all kinds of herbs and fruit trees which came from the mountains and from Babylonia.*

So the mystery continues. Some historians and archaeologists believe that the gardens did

Sculpted artwork from Nineveh that depicts hanging gardens

exist and were destroyed by war and erosion. Others believe earthquakes eventually leveled the gardens. Whether they were built in Babylon or Nineveh or nowhere at all, the Hanging Gardens remain the most mysterious of all the ancient wonders. Were they real or just a fabulous fantasy?

CHAPTER 3
The Temple of Artemis at Ephesus

King Croesus (say: KREE-suss) was known for his fabulous wealth. In fact, he was so wealthy that his name has come to *mean* wealth. Even today, people might say someone is "as rich as Croesus" to describe a billionaire.

While Croesus ruled Lydia (in present-day western Turkey), he often waged war on his Greek neighbors. But King Croesus also admired the Greeks—most of all, their art and architecture.

King Croesus

Sometime between 560 BC and 550 BC, Croesus conquered Ephesus, a Greek city on the coast of present-day Turkey. Shortly after his victory, he began the construction of many new buildings, including a great temple. Ancient Greek temples were built to house a statue of a god or goddess. The one that Croesus planned was to honor the goddess Artemis.

Artemis, Greek goddess of nature

Artemis was one of the most important goddesses to the Ephesians. They believed she had been born nearby. In Greece, Artemis was the goddess of hunting, wild animals, forests, and all of nature in general, although the people of Ephesus worshipped her mainly as a goddess of fertility.

The famous temple was begun about 550 BC. Pliny the Elder, a Roman historian, estimated that it took 120 years to complete. Of course, Croesus was long gone by then.

The Temple of Artemis was located outside the city in a park. Building it there made sense, since Artemis protected the natural world. The temple was enormous—425 feet long and 220 feet wide. It is believed to have had 127 columns that were 60 feet high, and the columns were each 4 feet in diameter. It was made of marble and thought to be the first Greek temple to be made out of that expensive stone.

The mammoth columns stood in a double row on all four sides. They rose like trees in a forest, towering over mere human beings. Approaching the temple must have been awe-inspiring for visitors. The outer row of columns were decorated with figures from Greek mythology carved into their bases.

Along the top of the temple, there was a decorative band showing more mythological scenes. All of this was painted in brilliant colors and trimmed with gold.

The temple's engineer and sculptor was named Theodorus. He set the foundation of the temple on marshy ground. That was so it would withstand earthquakes. Layers of sheepskin and packed charcoal helped support the massive weight of the temple.

When it was all completed, the temple was twice the size of other Greek temples.

Temple of Artemis

The Olympians

The ancient Greeks worshipped many gods and goddesses. Here are the main twelve, called the Olympians, because they lived on Mount Olympus.

- Aphrodite—Goddess of love, romance, and beauty
- Apollo—God of the sun, light, medicine, and music
- Ares—God of war
- Artemis—Goddess of the hunt and nature
- Athena—Goddess of wisdom and war
- Demeter—Goddess of farming
- Hephaestus—God of fire
- Hera—Queen of the goddesses, wife of Zeus
- Hermes—Messenger of the gods
- Hestia—Goddess of the home
- Poseidon—God of the sea
- Zeus—King of the gods, god of the sky

Zeus

As with many temples in ancient Greece, the temple at Ephesus was also the banking center of the city. Great sums of money were stored in a room called the treasury. So not only was the temple beautiful and imposing, it was also a symbol of wealth and power.

Also inside the temple was a statue of Artemis. The people of Ephesus would leave offerings and say prayers to her.

There were many temples dedicated to the goddess Artemis throughout the Greek world. However, the Ephesians considered the goddess to be *theirs*. The way they worshipped her proved their devotion. They had elaborate festivals in her honor. The goddess's image was carried through the streets, surrounded by maidens. The procession that led to the temple drew a huge crowd. Games, contests, and theatrical performances were held in the goddess's name.

The Parthenon

The temple at Ephesus may have been the largest built in the Greek style. But the Parthenon in Athens, Greece, is more famous. It was built about a hundred years after the Ephesus temple was begun. The Parthenon was dedicated to the goddess Athena. Originally, there was a huge statue of her inside.

The Parthenon in ancient times

Still standing, though in ruins now, the Parthenon is considered one of ancient Greece's greatest architectural accomplishments. Over seven million people visit it every year.

The Parthenon today

In Ephesus, businesses thrived, and the people grew rich. However, in the fourth century BC, the temple was destroyed by fire. Someone set it ablaze on purpose! He did it so he would become famous!

The temple was rebuilt on the same spot, with the same design, only smaller than the original. To make the temple seem bigger, it was built on a higher base. The Ephesians paid for the costs with their own jewelry. That's how important the temple was to them!

The temple was plundered by foreign invaders called Goths around AD 267. And although it was rebuilt once more, the temple was destroyed for good in the year 401.

Because of its fame, the Temple of Artemis was the very first ancient site that nineteenth-century Western archaeologists tried to find. It was finally discovered in 1869 by John Turtle Wood. Archaeologists found marble figures of Artemis and remains of the great temple.

Another excavation began in 1904. One of the most important discoveries was a carved column drum. (Columns were made by stacking these drums, one on top of another.) It is now in the British Museum.

The digs continue to the present day. Archaeologists are still looking for other traces of what was one of the greatest temples in the ancient world.

Temple of Artemis, present day

The British Museum

Located in London, England, the British Museum was founded in 1753. It contains a massive collection of fascinating objects from all periods in history. But many of the treasures, including those from ancient Greece, were taken without permission. For instance, between 1801 and 1812, Thomas Bruce,

Earl of Elgin, took some of the sculptures from the
Parthenon. Called the Elgin Marbles, they've been
on display in the British Museum since 1817. Today,
Greece is trying hard to get the museum to return
some of these works. But so far, the British Museum
has refused to give them back.

CHAPTER 4
The Statue of Zeus at Olympia

You have most probably watched the Summer Olympic Games on television. If so, you've been amazed by the swimmers and divers, runners and bike racers. But maybe you don't know that the Olympics started in Greece a long time ago— 776 BC, to be exact. Every four years, they were held at a shrine to Zeus—king of the Greek gods. (A shrine is a place considered holy, marked by some kind of building.) The shrine to Zeus was in a region called Peloponnesus (say: pel-uh-pohn-EE-suss).

As they do in our modern Olympics, athletes in ancient times traveled from near and far to compete. At that time, Greece wasn't one nation as it is today. It was made up of city-states. Often they were at war with each other. But during the Olympic Games, all the fighting stopped.

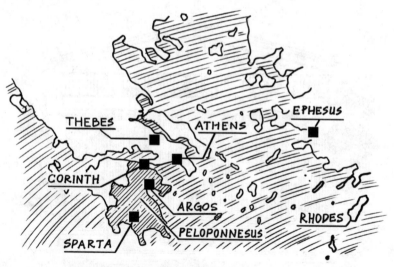

Greek city-states and Peloponnesus

The Olympics site was made up of a stadium, where the contests were held, and a sacred grove (an area of trees) where a number of temples stood. The shrine to Zeus was a simple one at first. But over time, as the games increased in importance, people felt that a new, large temple was needed.

The new temple was completed around 460 BC. It was similar to many other large Grecian temples, such as the Parthenon in Athens and the Temple of Artemis in Ephesus.

The temple was beautiful, but that is not what made it a wonder of the ancient world. It was the grand statue of Zeus inside that became so famous.

The sculptor chosen for this important task was Phidias (say: FID-ee-us). He had already completed a thirty-eight-foot-tall statue of the goddess Athena for the Parthenon in Athens. But the statue of Zeus was going to be bigger.

Phidias went to Olympia and set up a workshop. It would take him the next twelve years to complete the statue of Zeus.

Phidias

When it was finished, the statue was twenty-two feet wide and more than forty feet tall.

The figure of Zeus was shown sitting on a throne. His head nearly touched the roof of the temple. If he had been able to stand up, he would have broken right through it.

The statue was not made of marble or cast in metal. Instead, thin sheets of gold-plated bronze and ivory were attached to a wooden frame. Zeus's hair and sandals were made of gold. His robe, also gold, was carved with lilies and animals.

In his right hand, Zeus held a gold-and-ivory figure of Nike, the Greek goddess of victory. And in his left was a scepter—a decorated rod held by a ruler as a sign of power.

Nike, the Greek goddess of victory

The throne on which Zeus sat was adorned with gold, ebony (a rare tropical wood), and ivory. It was also studded with precious stones that came from faraway lands. Carved into the chair were figures of Greek gods and mythical animals, including a sphinx.

Ivory is hard to work with. It cracks easily. So once the statue was finished, the ivory parts were regularly rubbed with olive oil. The oil was kept in a pool in the floor of the temple. Light bounced off the pool from the doorway and may have had the effect of "spotlighting" the statue. For hundreds of years, tourists flocked to Olympia to gaze up at the breathtaking figure of the god.

The Lincoln Memorial

The Lincoln Memorial was built to honor Abraham Lincoln, the sixteenth president of the United States. It is located in Washington, DC, and was completed in 1922. The building is in the style of Greek temples such as the one at Olympia. And the larger-than-life-size statue of Lincoln is seated—showing he was a giant of a man just as Zeus was a giant of a god.

In 170 BC, an earthquake damaged the statue of Zeus, but it was repaired. Later, the Christian religion took hold in this part of the world. After AD 392, the Olympic Games were forbidden because they were seen as a pagan (non-Christian) custom and included what were considered pagan sacrifices.

So what happened to the statue of Zeus?

It was moved and became part of the collection of a wealthy Greek living in the city of Constantinople (now Istanbul). It's believed that the statue may have been destroyed by a fire that swept the city in 475. Smaller replicas of the statue were made, but none survive. Still, images found on ancient coins give clues about its appearance.

Not until 1829 was any excavation done. French archaeologists located the outlines of the temple. They found bits of sculpture, which they sent to the Louvre Museum in Paris. Next, Germans came in 1875. They worked at Olympia for five summers. They discovered still more fragments, and located the remains of the pool of oil in the floor.

Fragment from the Temple of Zeus in the Louvre Museum

Then, in the 1950s, an excavation discovered something that was very exciting—the workshop of Phidias. There were the sculptor's tools, a pit for casting bronze, clay molds, modeling plaster—even part of an elephant's tusk. It had supplied some of the ivory for the statue. Another thrilling discovery was a small bowl. On the bottom were these words: I BELONG TO PHIDIAS. This was a drinking cup that had once been the sculptor's!

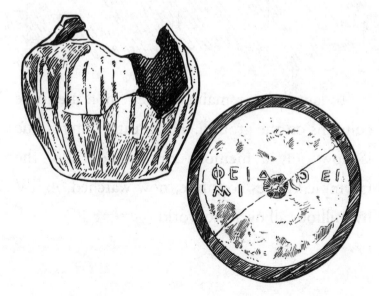

Today all that remains of the temple are some columns on the ground. The breathtaking statue is now only a memory. But, since 1896, the Olympic Games continue, now watched on TV by millions all over the world.

CHAPTER 5
The Mausoleum at Halicarnassus

The pharaohs of Egypt weren't the only rulers who spent vast amounts of time and money on their final resting place.

Mausolus (say: MAW-zuh-liss) ruled over Caria, an area in present-day Turkey. He also made sure that he had a grand tomb befitting his importance.

Mausolus ruled from 377 BC to 353 BC. He picked a new capital for Caria— the thriving city of Halicarnassus (say: ha-luh-kar-NA-suss).

Mausolus

Mausolus was a good ruler. He did a lot to promote prosperity. He oversaw the building of roads and city walls. He encouraged trade with other lands. And he also had taxes collected. So there was plenty of money to make his new capital city beautiful. He ordered the making of many fine marble statues, temples, and buildings.

But his grandest project was to be his own aboveground tomb. Although he was not Greek, Mausolus spoke Greek and admired Greek

culture. He chose two Greek architects to design his tomb.

When Mausolus died in 353 BC, his wife, Artemisia, saw to it that the work continued. She hired the most talented Greek artists of the day— one had been in charge of rebuilding the Temple of Artemis at Ephesus. She hired hundreds of other craftsmen, too. The magnificent tomb grew so famous that the king's name became the root of the word *mausoleum*. That means an aboveground building that houses a stately tomb.

The tomb was built on a hill that overlooked the city. It sat in an enclosed courtyard, on a stone platform. A staircase, flanked by stone lions, led to the entrance. Statues of gods and goddesses stood along the outer wall of the courtyard.

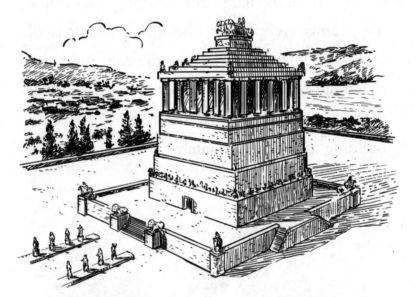

At each corner, stone warriors on horseback stood guard. Maybe these fierce warriors were meant to protect the tomb and the king who was laid to rest inside it.

The tomb was on top of a square tapered stone block that rose to about a third of the mausoleum's overall height of 140 feet. This base was covered with bas-relief sculpture that showed dramatic scenes from Greek mythology and history.

One part showed the battle between the Centaurs—mythical creatures who were half horse and half man—and the Lapiths, a legendary Greek people. Another showed Greeks in combat with the Amazons, a superstrong race of women.

Above this section of the tomb were thirty-six columns rising for about another 45 feet. In between each pair of columns was a statue. Behind the columns was a solid block of stone that bore the weight of the tomb's enormous roof.

The roof accounted for most of the final third of the mausoleum's height. It was in the form of a stepped pyramid. At the very top was a statue, believed to be of Mausolus and Artemisia sitting in a quadriga, a chariot pulled by four horses. A statue of this kind is also called a quadriga.

Bas-Relief

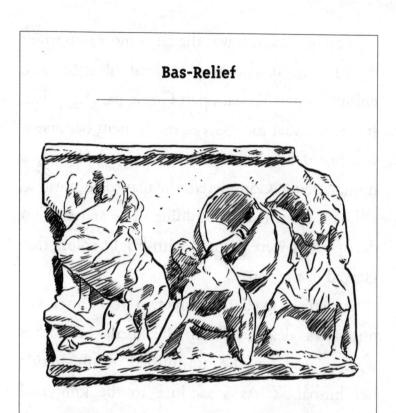

The word *bas-relief* means "low raised work." A bas-relief is a picture in stone that is only slightly carved out so that it rises from the stone's flat surface. Unlike a sculpture, no parts of bas-relief are fully three-dimensional.

The mausoleum was the city's most important monument. It also was a blend of styles and cultures—part Persian, part Greek, part Egyptian. It was unusual for a Greek monument because it was not dedicated to one of the gods, but to a human being. Completed, the mausoleum was as tall as a fifteen-story building. The statues that decorated it were painted with bright colors that glowed in the sun.

Artemisia lived for only two years after her husband's death. When she died, her ashes were placed in the unfinished tomb beside her husband's. As a sacrifice to the king and queen, dead animals were placed on the stairs leading to the tomb. Then the stairs were filled with stones and rubble so no one could get inside.

Despite repeated invasions of the city, the mausoleum stood for the next 1,700 years. But it could not withstand natural disasters. A series of earthquakes in the thirteenth century shattered the columns. The stone chariot crashed to the ground. By 1404, the mausoleum was barely recognizable.

Crusaders—Christian warrior-knights from Europe—were now occupying the region. They had little respect for monuments from ancient Greece. They hacked at the mausoleum's base and used the stones for their own building projects.

According to legend, around the year 1522, a group of Crusaders discovered a room inside the mausoleum one night. Deciding it was too late to explore it, they left. They returned the next day, eager to get their hands on whatever treasure might be inside. Imagine their shock and anger when they discovered . . . nothing! Someone had broken in and stolen everything. The Crusaders blamed the villagers or pirates. But it's possible that a few of the knights had returned the night before and were themselves the thieves.

In any case, the knights did not come away empty-handed. They took some of the tomb's finest remaining sculptures. They placed them in nearby Bodrum Castle, which had been built in the early fifteenth century. As for the other statues, the knights ground them up into lime that they used to make plaster.

In 1856, the British Museum sent the archaeologist Charles Thomas Newton to look for more remains of the mausoleum. This was a hard job. He didn't know the tomb's exact location. So Newton turned to the accounts of ancient writers for clues. Then he bought up the land that seemed to be in the most likely spot. When the dig got under way, Newton found walls, a staircase, and three of the corners of the foundation. The excavation went on for two years. His most remarkable discovery was the statues he believed to be of Mausolus and Artemisia. He also found other marble statues and pieces of the tomb. They were all sent to the British Museum.

Excavation of the Mausoleum at Halicarnassus

Today, Bodrum Castle still stands in Bodrum, Turkey. Polished stone and marble blocks that were built into the walls are still visible, reminders of the mausoleum's former glory. At the actual site of the mausoleum, only the foundation remains. The statues of Mausolus and Artemisia are still in the British Museum, where they preside over the remaining fragments—all that is left of the shining white marble tomb that Mausolus believed would honor him forever.

CHAPTER 6
The Colossus of Rhodes

Imagine you were a tourist in ancient times visiting a Greek island called Rhodes in the Mediterranean Sea. As your ship entered the harbor, you would have seen a gigantic figure of a man made of bronze standing in the bright sunlight.

(The statue's fingers alone were larger than most statues.) You would have had to tilt your head way back to see the top of his head. Who was this giant, and why was he there?

He was called the Colossus of Rhodes. A colossus is a larger-than-life statue. The Colossus of Rhodes represented the Greek sun god, Helios. Helios's sisters were Selene (goddess of the moon) and Eos (goddess of dawn). To the people of Rhodes, Helios was the most important god. He was honored with a major

Greek sun god, Helios

festival, as well as a series of games, much like the ancient Olympics.

The city of Rhodes was on the island of the same name. Because of its wealth and location on trade routes, foreign rulers often wanted to take it over. In 305–304 BC, Demetrius I of Macedon attacked Rhodes. He set up a blockade that lasted twelve months. (A blockade seals off a city to prevent goods or people from leaving or entering.) But the Rhodians wouldn't give up. So finally, Demetrius ended the blockade and left behind a lot of weapons and equipment. The people of Rhodes were able to sell all these things for a profit. Rhodes was already quite rich, so the leaders decided to spend this unexpected money on a massive statue that both honored their patron god and celebrated their resistance to Demetrius.

An artist named Chares (say: KAIR-eez) was chosen to sculpt the giant statue of Helios right by the harbor. The project took twelve years to complete. The statue was built from the ground up. It's likely that it was built on a base of sandstone blocks, which may have been set in a circle.

The bronze outer shell was probably applied in sheets and assembled right at the site. The shell was probably supported by iron struts inside. Certain parts, such as the legs, were weighted with stones to keep the figure from toppling over. Earth was piled around it to give the workers a platform. When the statue was done, the earth was carted away, leaving the gigantic statue standing alone.

Helios was believed to ride a chariot across the sky, pulling the sun behind him. But was this how Chares chose to depict him? We don't know for sure. Some silver coins of Rhodes show the god standing with his usual crown of pointed sunbeams. Perhaps the colossus resembled those images.

The statue has sometimes been shown with its legs spread wide on either side of the harbor so that ships could pass underneath. But no ancient account mentions that pose. And it seems unlikely the Greeks would have chosen this way to depict one of their gods—it wasn't very dignified! Also, such a pose would have meant shutting down the harbor during construction of the colossus. That would have stopped trade and cost the city a lot of money.

It's more likely that the colossus was posed in a more traditional Greek way, standing straight with both feet a small distance apart. Historians think the figure was nude or half-nude with a cloak over its left arm or shoulder. Some think it was wearing a spiked crown and shading its eyes from the rising sun with one hand. Or that it held a torch in the air, similar to the Statue of Liberty.

Statue of Liberty

On the base of the statue was this inscription:

To you, Helios, yes to you the people of Dorian Rhodes raised this colossus high up to the heaven, after they had calmed the bronze wave of war, and crowned their country with spoils won from the enemy. Not only over the sea but also on land they set up the bright light of unfettered freedom.

Where exactly the colossus stood is unknown. One possible location is the eastern side of the harbor. In medieval times it was said that the broken feet of the colossus once stood there.

Also near the harbor is a fortress. It was built much later using some finely carved blocks of marble. Why use such beautiful stone for a fortress? Some historians think that the marble blocks were the remains of a marble base for the colossus. Also, on the floor of the fortress is a circle of sandstone blocks. No one knows where they came from or why they are there.

Fort of St. Nicholas in Rhodes

The base of the colossus would probably have stood on sandstone blocks. So perhaps this is more evidence of the colossus's location.

Another possible location is in the center of the city. Ancient inscriptions and pieces of masonry (stonework from buildings) suggest that a temple to Helios may have once stood there. As we have seen with other wonders, such as the statue of Zeus, it was common for Greeks to place a statue of a god either in or next to the temple dedicated to that god. But many archaeological digs over many years have never turned up any signs of a giant statue there.

The Colossus remained standing until 226 or 225 BC, when an earthquake caused it to collapse. According to one Greek writer, the statue snapped at the knees and then lay in pieces on the docks because the locals believed that moving them would bring bad luck to the city. Even in fragments, the colossus must have inspired awe.

Around AD 654, a merchant bought the wreckage of the Colossus of Rhodes. It took nine hundred camels to cart away all that material. The once-glorious statue was melted down, reduced to nothing more than gleaming piles of scrap metal.

A New Colossus?

In the last fifty years, there has been talk of rebuilding the Colossus of Rhodes. In 2016, a group of European architects shared a plan to construct a new statue that would be 500 feet tall. That would make it five times taller than the original.

It would be covered in solar panels and built to withstand earthquakes and strong winds. The plan calls for the statue to be used as a cultural center and a lighthouse. The construction would create many jobs for workers, and the finished statue would bring lots of tourists to the island of Rhodes. So far, however, it's just a plan, not a reality.

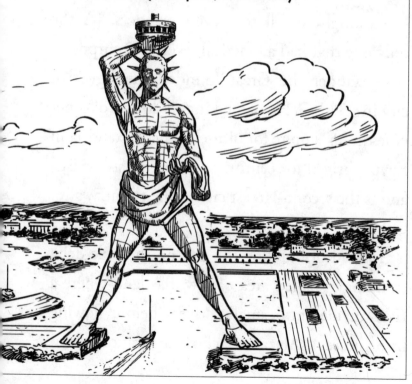

CHAPTER 7
The Lighthouse of Alexandria

In ancient times, the massive lighthouse on the island of Pharos, near the harbor of Alexandria, Egypt, was a beacon that guided ships to safety. Interestingly, of all the seven wonders, it's the only one that had a practical, everyday purpose.

Alexander the Great founded the Egyptian city in 332 BC. He named it and dozens of other cities in his empire for himself. The Alexandria in Egypt thrived for centuries. In fact, it still exists, and is the second-largest city in the country, after Cairo.

Instead of building the city on the Nile delta (a triangle-shaped area of low, flat land where a river divides into smaller rivers before flowing into the sea), Alexander chose a location about twenty miles west. He picked that site so that the mud and silt carried by the river wouldn't clog the city's two busy harbors.

After Alexander the Great died, work on the city was continued by Ptolemy I Soter (say: TOL-luh-mee SO-terr), Egypt's new ruler. Under Ptolemy, the city grew rich. Because of the many trade ships going in and out of the harbor, Ptolemy decided Alexandria needed a lighthouse. And in 270 BC, he gave the order to start building one. In today's money

Ptolemy I Soter

it cost three million dollars—an enormous sum for ancient times.

The lighthouse took twenty years to complete. By this time, Ptolemy I Soter had died, and his son, Ptolemy II, was the ruler of Alexandria.

Lighthouses

A lighthouse is a tower with a beacon. Now ships have GPS and other modern systems of navigation. However, for centuries, a fire from a lighthouse beacon helped ships coming into port avoid rocks, sandbars, and other dangers. Most lighthouses also included fog signals such as horns, bells, or cannons. If sailors couldn't see the light, they could still hear the warning sound.

Each lighthouse had a light "signature." For instance, a lighthouse might send out two flashes every three seconds, while another might send out four flashes every three seconds. Today, the tallest lighthouse in the world is the 436-foot lighthouse at Jeddah, which is located at the entrance to Jeddah Seaport in Saudi Arabia.

Lighthouse of Jeddah

Alexandria needed a lighthouse for practical reasons. The Egyptian coast was rocky and dangerous. Many Greek and Roman vessels were shipwrecked entering the city. A lighthouse could help prevent these tragedies.

But did Alexandria need such a big, fancy lighthouse?

No!

Ptolemy I and Ptolemy II (his son) wanted to advertise the city's greatness. Alexandria was not only a center for trade. It was also a city with a thriving arts scene, and known for advances in mathematics, astronomy, and medicine. The size of the lighthouse was meant to show off the city's grandeur and power.

It's said that Sostratus, a rich and powerful government official, designed the lighthouse. He had close ties with both Ptolemy I and Ptolemy II. Proud of his work, Sostratus wanted his name carved into the foundation of the lighthouse. The inscription said that the lighthouse had been built by Sostratus, ON BEHALF OF ALL MARINERS TO THE SAVIOR GODS. But Ptolemy II was not happy about this.

So the story goes that Sostratus had a new

inscription made in plaster. It covered over the old one. The new inscription gave the pharaoh credit for the lighthouse. That seemed to solve the problem. Only it didn't . . . and Sostratus knew it.

As time went by, the plaster chipped and fell off. The pharaoh's name could no longer be seen. But he was dead by that time, as was Sostratus. Only the inscription with Sostratus's name lived on for the ages—just as Sostratus had planned.

The lighthouse stood at the eastern end of the island of Pharos, which was a short distance from the coast. It was built of limestone from a quarry nearby. Limestone, however, is a soft stone, and not the best choice for a lighthouse. So certain parts of the building, as well as the door and window frames, were reinforced with granite.

There are two detailed descriptions of the lighthouse, given much later, by travelers in the tenth century. According to these accounts, the building was three hundred cubits high. Because the cubit measurement varied from place to place, however, this could mean that the lighthouse stood anywhere between 450 and 600 feet high. That means it was at least as tall as a forty-story building. Compare its height to another famous landmark that is in a harbor—the Statue of Liberty. Lady Liberty certainly looks like a giant, and yet she is only 151 feet high (on her pedestal, 305 feet).

Unlike most modern lighthouses, which are built as tapering columns, the Pharos lighthouse was probably blockier—almost like an ancient skyscraper. And it was probably white, so that it would be easily visible to sailors.

The lighthouse was made up of three sections, each one stacked on top of another. The lowest level, which sat on a high stone platform, was like a giant box. The door to this section wasn't at the bottom, but partway up, and was reached by a 600-foot-long ramp on the outside.

Inside was a large spiral ramp. It was wide enough for oxen to carry wood toward the top of the lighthouse. A series of windows allowed light to come in.

The next section was shaped like an octagon, an eight-sided figure. This level had about fifty rooms. Some were used for the staff who kept the fire burning at the top. Others were for storing wood.

The third and final level of the lighthouse was shaped like a giant cylinder—think of a great big can. It was too narrow for a ramp, so they included a staircase. When the oxen reached this point, they had to stop. Workers had to do the rest of the carrying.

On top of the cylinder was an open cupola. (A cupola is a small dome that sits on top of a roof or ceiling.) This was where the fire burned that provided the light. According to

Cupola

ancient accounts, a large curved mirror, maybe of polished bronze, was used to project the fire's light into a beam. But some scholars have doubted this story.

At the very top of the lighthouse was a statue. In Greek times, this was probably a bronze image of either the god Poseidon or Helios.

During the day, the smoke from the ever-burning fire guided the boats. At night, the flames did the job. It was said ships could see the light or the smoke from one hundred miles away.

Poseidon, Greek god of the sea

Even in ancient times, the lighthouse was a tourist attraction. Vendors sold food to visitors on the platform at the top of the first level. For those who wanted to climb still higher, there was a smaller balcony that offered spectacular views of the sea from the top of the eight-sided tower.

The lighthouse stood for over 1,600 years, even surviving a giant tidal wave that hit the eastern Mediterranean in AD 365. But by the end of the tenth century, cracks became visible. At that point, the lighthouse underwent a restoration that lowered the height of the building by about seventy feet.

Then, on August 8, 1303, a major earthquake shook the region. A third of Alexandria was destroyed, and the lighthouse was seriously damaged. The final collapse came in 1375. Ruins remained on the site until 1480, when much of the building's stone was used to build a fortress on the island of Pharos that still stands today.

Of the Seven Wonders of the Ancient World that have vanished, the Lighthouse of Alexandria is probably the one for which we have the best record. Several coins have been found that show images of it. Mosaics (pictures on floors or walls made of small tiles) of the lighthouse have also been discovered. One is from the year AD 539, and it shows the lighthouse during Greek times, with a statue at the top. Still another mosaic is in Venice, Italy, at the famous Basilica of St. Mark.

Mosaic in the Basilica of St. Mark
that depicts the Lighthouse of Alexandria

For a long time it was known that pieces of the lighthouse had to be at the bottom of the port of Alexandria. But it was not until recently that anyone considered looking for them.

Underwater excavations began in 1968, stopped, and then started up again in the 1990s. Divers found large blocks of stone that certainly seem to have come from a huge building. They also found statues that may have stood at the base.

Today, the whole area is an underwater park. Tourists with diving gear can swim around the remains of the great Lighthouse of Alexandria, all that's left of the "wonder" that was once such an important part of life in the city.

CHAPTER 8
The Wonders through the Ages

All but one of the Seven Wonders have been destroyed. They were famous landmarks in a world long gone. Yet the memory of them has inspired artists, architects, builders, and planners throughout the ages, and they still have meaning today. Without modern tools, materials, or resources, people of ancient times found ways to create extraordinary monuments.

The idea of listing worldwide wonders has continued. In the nineteenth and early twentieth centuries, some writers made lists that included buildings and monuments from later times or from other parts of the world. Between 2000 and 2007, a contest was held "to select a new Seven Wonders of the World." More than one hundred million people voted, and they chose these structures as the winners:

- The Colosseum in Rome, Italy
- The Great Wall of China
- Chichen Itza, Mexico
- Machu Picchu, Peru
- Christ the Redeemer, Rio de Janeiro, Brazil
- Petra, Jordan
- The Taj Mahal, India

Machu Picchu, Peru

Then there are natural wonders, such as the Grand Canyon in Arizona, and these others:

- Aurora Borealis, or Northern Lights (They can be seen in Alaska, northern parts of Canada, the southern half of Greenland, Iceland, northern Norway, Sweden, and Finland.)

Aurora Borealis

- Victoria Falls, on the border between Zambia and Zimbabwe
- Mount Everest, in China and Nepal
- Paricutin Volcano, Mexico
- The Great Barrier Reef, Australia
- Harbor of Rio de Janeiro, Brazil

Now that you know all about the wonders both ancient and more modern, make a list of the ones you think are the most remarkable. Who knows—maybe you'll get to visit them one day!

Timeline for the Seven Wonders
of the Ancient World

c. 2550–2530 BC	Construction of the Great Pyramid at Giza
550 BC	Construction of Temple of Artemis at Ephesus begins
c. 435 BC	Statue of Zeus constructed
356 BC	Temple of Artemis at Ephesus destroyed by fire; later rebuilt
353 BC	Mausoleum of Halicarnassus built
270 BC	Ptolemy I orders building of the Lighthouse of Alexandria
c. 226 BC	Colossus of Rhodes toppled by an earthquake
170 BC	Earthquake damages the statue of Zeus at Olympia; later repaired
AD 401	Temple of Artemis at Ephesus destroyed
654	Merchant buys the bronze wreckage of the Colossus of Rhodes
1375	Final collapse of the Lighthouse of Alexandria
1829	Excavation begins on Temple of Zeus at Olympus
1869	Temple of Artemis at Ephesus discovered
1880	Excavation begins on the Great Pyramid
1968	Excavation of the Lighthouse of Alexandria begins

Timeline of the World

2575–2130 BC	Old Kingdom of Egypt
1539–1075 BC	New Kingdom of Egypt
776 BC	Olympic Games begin in Greece
753 BC	Founding of Rome
509 BC	Creation of Roman Republic
480–323 BC	Classical period of ancient Greece
447–432 BC	Parthenon built
31 BC–27 BC	Roman Republic destroyed
AD 306	Constantine becomes emperor
410	Fall of Rome
1260	Chartres Cathedral completed in France
1492	Christopher Columbus sails to the New World
1517	Martin Luther's Ninety-Five Theses begin the Protestant Reformation
1753	British Museum founded in London, England
1775	American Revolution begins
1808	Napoleon conquers northern Italy
1896	Olympic Games start again
1968	Summer Olympic Games held in Mexico City

Bibliography

*Books for young readers

Cartwright, Mark. "Colossus of Rhodes." *Ancient History Online*,
  July 25, 2018, https://www.ancient.eu/Colossus_of_Rhodes.

Cartwright, Mark. "Temple of Artemis at Ephesus." *Ancient History
  Online*, July 26, 2018, https://www.ancient.eu/Temple_of_
  Artemis_at_Ephesus.

Dalley, Stephanie. *The Mystery of the Hanging Garden of
  Babylon.* New York: Oxford University Press, 2015.

Ducksters, "Ancient Greece for Kids." https://www.ducksters.com/
  history/ancient_greece.php.

*Macaulay, David. *Pyramid.* Boston: Houghton Mifflin, 1975.

*MacDonald, Fiona. *I Wonder Why Greeks Built Temples:
  And Other Questions about Ancient Greece.* New York:
  Kingfisher Books, 1997.

Mark, Joshua J. "Great Pyramid of Giza." *Ancient History Online*,
  December 19, 2016, https://www.ancient.eu/Great_Pyramid_
  of_Giza.

"Mausoleum of Halicarnassus." *Encyclopaedia Britannica Online.*
  Last modified August 23, 2017. https://www.britannica.com/
  topic/Mausoleum-of-Halicarnassus.